MW01385797

THE GRASS IS GREENER

Jez Alborough

A & C BLACK · LONDON

Once upon a farm there lived a flock of sheep whose leader was called Thomas. One morning, while the others were busily chomping their breakfasts, Thomas moaned, "This grass is no good."

One by one everyone agreed with him.

Except a lamb called Lincoln.

He was far too busy chasing butterflies.

"Let's climb up that hill," said Thomas. "The grass at the top looks much greener than ours."

And everyone agreed.

Except Lincoln.

He was far too busy
jumping with the rabbits.

So they left without him.

They climbed up,

and up,

and up.

But when they reached the top . . .

they found that the grass up there . . .

"Goodness!" said Thomas quickly. "What a wonderful view. From up here we could find the greenest field in the *whole country!*"

And everyone agreed.
So they looked round,
        and round,
            and round . . .

getting dizzier,
  and dizzier,
    and dizzier . . .

until, suddenly, Thomas stopped.
"Look, look!" he bleated.
"There it is, the greenest field
in the whole country!"

So they climbed down . . .

until, finally, they reached the bottom.

"Hello," said Lincoln.
"Where have you all been?"
"Oh . . . Us?" panted Thomas.
"Er . . . Nowhere special. We . . .
    er . . . just went for a little walk . . .
    Didn't we . . .?"

And of course . . .

Everyone agreed.

Except Lincoln.

He was far too busy enjoying his lunch.

Dedicated to Lincolns everywhere

First published 1987 by A & C Black (Publishers) Ltd,
35 Bedford Row, London WC1R 4JH.

Copyright © 1987 Jez Alborough

British Library Cataloguing in Publication Data
Alborough, Jez
The grass is greener
I. Title
823'.914   [J]   PZ7

ISBN 0–7136–2809–X

Phototypeset in Bembo Infant by Kalligraphics Limited
Printed by South China Printing Co., Hong Kong